God's Arm Is Not Too Short

God's Arm *is* Not too Short

Cynthia L. Nichols

XULON ELITE

Xulon Press Elite
555 Winderley Pl, Suite 225
Maitland, FL 32751
407.339.4217
www.xulonpress.com

© 2024 by Cynthia L. Nichols

All rights reserved solely by the author. The author guarantees all contents are original and do not infringe upon the legal rights of any other person or work. No part of this book may be reproduced in any form without the permission of the author.

Due to the changing nature of the Internet, if there are any web addresses, links, or URLs included in this manuscript, these may have been altered and may no longer be accessible. The views and opinions shared in this book belong solely to the author and do not necessarily reflect those of the publisher. The publisher therefore disclaims responsibility for the views or opinions expressed within the work.

Unless otherwise indicated, Scripture quotations taken from the King James Version (KJV)–*public domain*.

Paperback ISBN-13: 978-1-66289-160-1
Hardcover ISBN-13: 978-1-66289-266-0
Ebook ISBN-13: 978-1-66289-161-8
Audiobook ISBN-13: 978-1-66289-162-5

Dedication

To God who trustingly called me to write for Him. Who dries my tears and heals my hurts. Thank you.

To my husband for his patience and loving endurance through coping with the tears and grief that surfaced while writing my stories.

Thank you both for walking through this with me. To God be all the glory!

God is our refuge and strength, a very present help in times of trouble.

Psalm 46:1 (KJV)

The Lord of hosts is with us; the God of Jacob is our refuge. Selah.

Psalm 46:7 (KJV)

Be still and know that I am God: I will be exalted among the heathen, I will be exalted in all the earth.

Psalm 46:10 (KJV)

Note From the Author

The writing of this book is the fulfilling of my life's dream. To be used by God is my highest calling and desire. When God told Frank to tell me to write, I was excited and honored. God gave me the strength and insight to write as His Holy Spirit revealed the hidden answers to my past questions of, "God, where are You?" I invite you to walk with me through my true stories and see the amazing ways God was and still is present and faithful in every step of my journey.

Though our hurts and circumstances may differ, my hope and prayer for you is to learn to truly trust in God as I have. My past was God's boot camp for me, preparing me for the purpose He designed me for. I realize I am His conduit of healing to a lost and hurting world. I want my readers to be able to find real purpose and value through the stories of their own lives. The gifts of giving and receiving forgiveness. The freedom of real life and self-worth that comes only from our Lord and Savior, Jesus

Christ. Enjoy living in God's love. Keep watching for God moments and everyday miracles.

Blessings,
Cindy

Table of Contents

1. God's Wonders at Work............................1
2. The Oregon Fire of 2020.........................5
3. The Oregon Ice Storm of 2022....................9
4. God is Alive in the Storms of Life..............15
5. A New Beginning After the Storm................23
6. Parental Concerns Never Cease..................29
7. God's Hand in Unexpected Blessings..............31
8. Daily Blessings Can Often be Overlooked.........35
9. God Shows Up in Unexpected Places...............39
10. The Power of Prayer is Always Active............43
11. From Tragedies to Blessings.....................47
12. God Sends His Angels to Guard Us................51
13. Seeking God Has Great Rewards...................55
14. God's Protection is With Us Wherever We Go.....57
15. God Turned a Crash into a Blessing..............59
16. Watching God Working Strongly in My Family.....61
17. When God Calls, He Provides.....................65
18. Jesus's Example of Trust in His Father..........69

Acknowledgements....................................73
About the Author....................................79

- 1 -

God's Wonders at Work

How does God put life together? With so many quirks, it is difficult to fathom how His purpose and plan come together so perfectly.

I accepted Jesus as my Savior when I was eight years old. Little did I know at that age that He always kept me safe. Once, when my brother and I went to the park, a scary looking woman sat on a bench near me. Turns out she was a fortune teller, and she grabbed my hand to read my palm. I tried to pull away, but she hung onto me and told me I would die at an early age. Being eight and scared, I jerked away, took my brother's hand, and ran home. We had no dad at home, so I was expected to keep him safe.

A couple of years later when I was ten, a man mother knew came to see her. I had a foreboding feeling about him and did not trust him. He drove an old-fashioned bread van with racks on both sides and a center aisle. The passenger's door was controlled by the driver. He was going on a bread run and Mom forced me to go with him. After we left Mom, I felt very uneasy. He had some doughnuts in the van and I cautiously asked if I could have one. He got very angry and shoved a maple bar in my mouth. He nearly choked me! I could hardly breathe! I was so frightened I wanted to cry, but I knew better.

The man turned onto a secluded road in the mountains, saying he had a delivery to make. When he came to a gate, he said, "Oh, they are not home," and turned the van around. After driving downhill to a secluded area away from any houses, he parked on the side of the road. I asked him why we were stopping. He said, "To cool my brakes." That did not sound right. The next thing I knew, he had me out of my seat and was forcing me to lie on my back in the center aisle. He began drawing on my body with ink… I learned later they were Satanic symbols. That is when I noticed some black plastic and a dirty shovel under the shelving. I asked him what it was for, but he brushed off my question. I asked him what he was doing when he began to undo his clothes, but before anything happened, he was quickly putting me back in my seat. He heard a car; it was a police car! The man warned me not to say anything or he would do something drastic to me.

I tried to look as frightened as I felt when the officer asked me if I was all right. The evil man was staring at my face with so much intensity. I wanted to scream, "No! I am trapped!", but all I could do was silently nod. When the officer drove away, I prayed the scary man would take me back to my mother. He did. Before he let me go, he warned me not to tell anyone what had happened or else he would hurt my mother.

The moment I was out of the van, I ran into the house and locked myself in the bathroom. This was my usual practice when I was afraid. Mom's friend, Lois, noticed and told Mom something was wrong. Mom asked if I was all right. Fearfully, I lied and said, "Yes." I stayed in the bathroom for a long time trying to wash the ink off of my body to no avail. When I came out of my safe place, I cautiously peeked out the window to see if the man was gone. He was still there talking to Mom. At that point, I lost all respect for my mother.

As an adult, I realized my healing process would begin only through forgiveness. I knew in my heart I had to personally forgive the man and pray for his salvation. No way did I want to spend eternity with that man. If I wanted to be free, I had to have a forgiving heart. Jesus died for him as well as for me. If he accepted Jesus as his Savior, God could change him. If not, God could punish him better than I ever could. That was my solace.

It took years of working hand in hand with my Lord in obedience. Sharing my story is the final step in my healing. I also forgave Mom for making me go and for not being there for me. Now, I am free. I hope others find healing from my story.

- 2 -

The Oregon Fire of 2020

According to an Oregon forest ranger I spoke with who worked for the Oregon Department of Forestry, approximately one million acres were burned during the Oregon Fire of 2020. This was a fire of historic proportion for the state of Oregon. More than 10 percent of the population had to evacuate for their own safety. Those were considered the Labor Day wildfires. The state fairgrounds in Salem became the emergency rescue center. There were several other rescue centers, as well.

Many quilters throughout Oregon made quilts to give to those who lost their homes in the fire. They were taken to a designated place for distribution. Many friends and family members housed or made room for motor homes that survived the fire. There were so many who died and those who managed to escape were traumatized. The fire and police departments were priceless assets in rescue and counseling in all areas needed. God's hand was there in saving lives and rescuing people, animals, and homes.

Fires can create their own weather including fire tornadoes. When this happens, the fire can jump over a home and devastate the next home, leaving the neighboring home untouched. Many people whose homes were not touched stood in awe, some realizing the hand of God at work and others in amazement and wonder with a lot of questions. My husband and I were privileged to have one such family over for dinner. Their home was spared from damage, even from smoke damage as the fire came up to their fence and around them. For me, I could see how God's arm directed the fire.

Several people made room for many animals that needed rescuing while other rescues of people and means of survival were taking place. The heart of God is visible through the loving hands of others. The loss of life and animals is always too devastating to talk about, and I would not want to traumatize those who may be reading this book. Many are still recovering from the trauma to this day.

I was especially touched by a man who was our guest for dinner. I noticed he had two carved bear heads in his truck he had rescued from his home. To my surprise, he could not stand to see them burned in the fire. I had a carved bear on my front porch that matched them. He was planning to stop over before they were to leave our neighbor's house so I could give mine to him, but instead, he gave me his and refused to take my bear. It is difficult to receive a gift from someone who was not sure there would be anything left at his home, but he was a proud man who was receiving help and must have felt pretty humbled.

God showed me the other side of giving and receiving through this interaction. By accepting the man's gift when he was in need, I was able to hopefully give back some of his dignity. This was a God lesson for me in the many ways to lend a helping hand. I hope to be a better and more sensitive person for learning it.

- 3 -

The Oregon Ice Storm of 2022

In 2022, Oregon had an ice storm of historic proportion. I was amazed at the hand of God at work. All through the night, the temperatures plummeted to below freezing. My husband and I had five acres surrounded by forest and a meadow. The freezing rain blanketed the trees and most everything around us. We could hear tree after tree crack and fall all around our house. My neighbors had been watching the trees fall on our property and called to see if we were all right. We assured them we were.

There were so many trees falling that it was difficult to know where they were. We prayed for safety and went to sleep. We were awakened to people talking followed by the sound of chainsaws. I heard the people say that our yard looked like a war zone. When my husband and I looked outside, we were shocked at what we found. We had lost over thirty-five trees and still had to take out ten more for safety. God's grace of good neighbors was amazing. Five guys with chainsaws came to clear our driveway so we could get out. We also found that a huge tree had fallen on our roof and caused damage to our deck. Our fences were smashed and everything was encased in ice, including our car.

My husband was recovering from surgery, so I went outside to help clear some of the debris. When I came back inside, I called our insurance company right away. They were already overloaded from the snow and ice storms all over the country. I was so glad God gave me the foresight to call them right away because it put us in the cue with others needing help. It was difficult to find inspectors and workers who could help us. Our neighbors helped us by covering our roof so we would not incur more water damage. My husband and I prayed daily for God's provision and gave praise for our safety and all He was going to do for us through this journey.

It took several months to get everything repaired. The toughest part was getting our roof fixed. The company that made the tiles for our old roof no longer existed along with the actual tile we needed. The insurance company helped us search all over the United States for tile to match and were not able to find any. Finally, the insurance agreed to put on an equivalent in cost and God blessed us with a metal roof. Wow! Beyond our wildest dreams.

Much of the debris from the cleanup was burned in small piles. Habitat for Humanity, a company we used every year, came and cleaned up the fallen trees and underbrush. I was hoping the worker would make smaller piles, but he did not. I could see he was exhausted from the many hours he had already worked cleaning up for so many. I was left with a massive pile of stumps, all manner of underbrush, and trees. Frank and I measured the burn pile and it was 35 by 25 feet wide, 15 feet high.

The weather was getting hotter and I needed to get this pile burned before the burn date was cut off. The day came when burning was permitted. Frank was going to check with the weather report to see if the winds were down enough to burn safely. I checked with the fire department and told them the dimensions of the pile, but they would not burn it for me. After all of the fires in our area recently, I was very reluctant to burn this pile of debris safely. I told Frank I did not want to hear from the weather report, I wanted to hear from God. Frank prayed and God answered him, saying, "My arm is not too short." That was enough for me, so we started the fire. Then Frank went up to the upper lawn where the wood was being cut for firewood.

We were blessed to have a crew of seven men from the Adult & Teen Challenge, a faith-based rehab center, help bring logs up from the meadow full of downed trees. This global rehab center, founded by David Wilkerson, has chapters all across the United States and is based on Christian values to help those struggling with addiction to find hope and healing through discipleship.

While Frank and the men cut trees, I was left to burn the huge pile alone with a garden hose nearby just in case. At one point, the flames grew so tall that the guys stopped working and said the flames were 40 feet above our house. The base of the fire was at least 20 feet below our house (we live on a side hill in a split-level home). I was sitting on the ground about 20 feet from the fire. It was very hot, but I did not get burned. I thanked God for being there with me and for His help. I asked God to move the flame around the pile so it would not go through the pile and catch the forest to my right on fire. He did! Then I asked Him to do the same on the left side of the pile. The flame was extremely tall and about 5 feet in diameter. That is when He moved the flame around the fire toward where I was sitting. God laid the huge flame down and sent it through the bottom of the pile.

The flame swirled around and burned the pile to the ground in a matter of seconds. I was awestruck with wonder at the mighty hand of God at work. This was a faith-building experience I needed to see firsthand. God's mighty arm truly is not too short for fires or any other thing or situation that seems impossible to reach. He is almighty God, and at that moment, I became more than a believer. I became a knower of God's power. He hears me when I call and truly cares enough to answer in His very timely manner. I can only praise Him and thank Him. Wow!

While all of this was going on, God gave me an added blessing. Between where I sat and the blazing fire was a beehive. Suddenly, a whole colony of tiny colorful bees swarmed out of it. They were very beautiful and unlike any bee I had ever seen. They were the size of a medium-sized straight pinhead and were a florescent green and gold with black eyes encircled in gold. They looked like curious tiny aliens floating around me. They were as curious as I was. It was as though they came with God's hand. I looked online to see if I could find a photo of one, but was unsuccessful. Wherever they came from, the bees were friendly and fun to watch. When the fire was out, the bees were gone just as quick. What an amazing treat!

I was so very blessed to see the hand of God work on my behalf. His arm was mighty, timely, and accurate, just as it is in our lives, even when we may not recognize it at the time.

- 4 -

God is Alive in the Storms of Life

As a teenager, life was pretty tough as it is for many others. I was sixteen when a marriage proposal came my way and it sounded like a new life, a change which I thought could improve my life… That was not the reality at all.

First of all, I did not know that a Christian was not to be unequally yoked with an unbeliever. I always thought the dad in the family was the one to give permission to marry, so I asked mine. He said yes and that he would sign for me. I asked him to walk me down the aisle, but he refused and said he was washing his hands of me. That was a shock. I knew he did not think I was his child, but I did not know he disliked me that much.

What I had seen of Dad growing up was very little. I remember my aunt lived in the same apartment building a few doors down and my dad was there playing with her twins, so I went to him (I was about four years old at the time). When I got there, he told me to go home where I belonged. I said I belonged with my daddy, but he took me to the door and sent me home crying. This all came back when he told me he was washing his hands of me. I was a daddy's girl in my heart and could never accept that kind of rejection.

When I married my first husband, it was not long before my eyes began to open. Within the first eighteen months of marriage, I had a miscarriage. I was hospitalized because only part of my baby came out. The rest had to be taken out surgically. I did not know the medical term for this kind of surgery was abortion. When the nurse came in and asked me if I was the one who had an abortion, I said, "No, I just had a miscarriage." To this day, I do not call it an abortion. I did not kill my baby as is the connotation today. That was devastating. My baby died in the womb; it was hard enough to have half of my dead baby still inside my body. To top it all off, my husband told me later when I was crying that, "It was not a baby anyway." Where was the love? The caring compassion? I knew marriage was a forever commitment and I was determined to make the marriage work. He continued to drink and make fun of my faith.

We had been married for about fifteen years when his brother and sister-in-law came to Oregon where we lived. Over time, she and I became best friends. I was pretty naive even then. I had just gone through a serious surgery when he took us and our two children to his brother's so he could help my sister-in-law with some wallpapering in her kitchen. I lay on the couch trying to rest while they worked and enjoyed each other's company. We stayed a couple of days while they finished.

One evening, we were watching TV together and I noticed my husband watching my sister-in-law sewing. He looked so content when he turned to me and asked, "Why can't you be more like her?" I told him I sewed a lot, too, for I made most of my children's clothes. That was heartbreaking to me, but I just tried to keep doing better. I always tried to do the right thing and not make waves.

A surprising day came when my sister-in-law, my best friend, had boxed up everything I had ever given her over the years and gave it back to me. I had no idea why or what happened. Everything seemed all right between us. She never did say anything to me about it. The next day, she and my husband went to her babysitter's house. They went to get some of the babysitter's wash (my sister-in-law had been doing her wash for her). I asked if I could go with them, but my husband said no. They were gone a very long time and the babysitter gave me a knowing look... We were thinking the same thing.

They went again the next day, so this time, I went looking for them. I found them at an A&W sitting snugly together in the car. I came up to the passenger's door and told her, "Get out. I want to sit by my husband."

She said, "No. I was just talking to him about his brother," who was her husband.

Then I told my husband to tell her to move, but he did not. I left them there with thoughts of packing up our kids and going home. I was still too weak to take care of them yet.

I used to always fix my husband's breakfast and coffee before he went to work, but when my sister-in-law divorced her husband, mine started going to her house for coffee. I went, too. When I confronted them, my sister-in-law, her boyfriend's daughter, and my husband began taunting and making fun of me.

I gave my marriage all I could. My husband began meeting her at the donut shop and chuckled when I wanted him to come and get me. I was the babysitter for what turned out to be their rendezvous. With the kids in bed and asleep, I lay on the couch and cried my heart out, not knowing what to do. One day, I found them at the donut shop together. She had already admitted to them having an affair. I asked her to leave so I could talk to my husband. She refused. I told my husband to make her leave so I could talk to him. He refused. I asked him if he was in love with her in front of her. He said, "Not like you think." Then I confronted him about their affair and he asked me where I had heard that. I looked at her and told him she had told me. He did not deny it. I told him I guessed he made his choice and left.

It was not long after that I became suicidal. I did not want that. I had two kids to finish raising. I had gone to a counseling session and was on my way home when a car ran a stop sign and broadsided me. I was in the hospital for about a week because I was unable to walk. I had not left him yet; I was still home with my kids and husband. I begged him to go to counseling to no avail.

I came home from the hospital on Christmas Eve and had to shop at a 7-Eleven for gifts, though my children's best Christmas present was having me home. I could not leave the marriage at Christmas time. I tried to make him leave and go where he was happy, but he would not leave. I did the best I could at restoring our marriage, but it was not a one-person task. It takes two to make a marriage, and I could not do it alone.

I finally made the decision to get help. I was getting more despondent and needed to get away to stay safe because suicide definitely was not the answer. I went to the state hospital to see if they could help me. They said I was not crazy and said no. I knew I had to get help away from him, so I told them I was afraid I would commit suicide if they did not help me. As dumb as it sounds, it was better than leaving my children motherless.

I was finally admitted and stayed there for three months. During that time, my children were at home with their dad. At the time, I never realized how difficult it would be for my children to come and visit me at the hospital. While there, my husband was sleeping with another friend with my children still in the house. His brother told me to find a safe place for my daughter because he found out that her dad, my husband, was playing peeping Tom on her when she went to the bathroom. The police were informed, but could not do anything because they did not have proof. She went to live with my friend until I got home. I had no idea that my son was being mistreated by his dad until many years later.

An event happened in the hospital that showed me how God was using this experience for my growth. When I was being admitted, I had to have a physical. The doctor was inappropriate and the nurse was there to witness it. I was taken to join a panel of those who were in charge of the hospital. There, I was asked many questions about what happened and the nurse verified my answers. The doctor had a chance to explain his side. In the end, the doctor was fired. People who do not work in state institutions or hospitals of this kind seldom know what really goes on when the staff keep quiet in order to save their jobs.

- 5 -

A New Beginning After the Storm

When I got out of the hospital, I was told that if I went back into the same situation I had come out of that I would end up back in there. I also found out that because I had been in their program that I qualified to get into a program at Chemeketa Community College where I could continue my education. I did not have anything I could call a resume as I had dropped out of school after getting married and had only ever been a wife and mother. I tried to stay in school because I only had one year until graduation, but my husband did not want me to continue. We moved too often and changing schools so often became a problem.

I checked out the Chemeketa Community College and enrolled in the GED program. I graduated with my GED and continued on to get my associate's degree in psychology. I also took some classes in electronics. After graduation, I looked for a job in electronics until I could set up my own practice as a counselor. I needed more insight and business experience to achieve that goal. I stayed at the women's center at Union Gospel Mission for a while. The vocational rehab center helped me get into an apartment and finish my degree. After having been in the hospital, I was directed to the vocational rehab center and they agreed to help me as long as I was in school. I focused on school and getting through the process of divorce and healing. It was very helpful that I was taking psychology.

In the meantime, I met my future husband, Frank, at a divorce recovery class at the church he was attending. All of the attendees were hurting and we were asked to introduce ourselves to those around us and make them feel welcome. I showed him where the refreshment table was, but he was not interested in receiving my assistance. At the end of the evening class, I told him the restaurant the class would meet at so we could get better acquainted. To my surprise, he showed up. We talked, and several months later, I invited him over to play a game of Chinese checkers, which I discovered later he hated. We began dating and were married about a year and a half later after I graduated from Chemeketa Community College.

Frank and I were still newlyweds, but he encouraged me to achieve my goals and better myself as much as I wanted to. He always encouraged me to succeed in everything I did. After thirty-five years of marriage, I am still his forever bride and he is my forever sweetheart husband. He is my blessing from God.

By God's grace, I received a settlement from a car accident. I asked Frank if I could use the money I received to finish my education. He agreed. It had been a dream of mine to finish high school and go to college. I did. The remote dream that had seemed so impossible to me was to attend a Christian college. I felt like God had just handed me a huge miracle when the settlement came in and Frank agreed to let me enroll at Western Baptist College to get my bachelor's degree in psychology and family studies.

I enrolled in the adult studies program called family studies, an intense two-year program. Frank, being a teacher, agreed to critique my papers for spelling and punctuation. He was a much better typist than I was and was a great help. For God to give me such a godly man to marry who was and is so unselfish was a blessing I never knew would ever be mine.

God can reach to the lowest depths and heal the deepest hurts imaginable. Years of hurt and agonizing emotional pain were being healed through the psychology classes I took. All class group discussions consisted of a classroom of psychologists who could see into the heart of the matter. None of us could get away without dealing with issues that could pose a problem in the lives of themselves and others when we were working with potential clients. We cannot really help others with their problems if ours are lurking in the background.

Wow! God really knows how to reach into the depths of our seemingly impossible situations. Not only did God fulfill my greatest dreams, He also began healing my deepest hurts. He helped me to forgive those who had hurt me over the years. The first step was to ask God to give me a heart to forgive. Then, I would pray daily for them individually until the pain went away. Without true forgiveness from my heart, I could not experience and understand the depths of God's forgiveness for me. Forgiveness frees the one who was hurt, not the one who has done the hurting. That person or persons have to seek their own forgiveness from God or face their own consequences. Praise God I am free.

I wanted to continue my education by getting my doctorate in psychology. I started taking classes at George Fox College, but I ran out of money. I also had surgery and was unable to work. So now, I work for the Lord whenever He sends someone my way. The pay is not in money, but in helping those in need to find healing. The benefits are out of this world and eternal. To God be all the glory!

There are many miracles throughout these stories. The police officer showing up when he did when I was a child. The man taking me back to my mother. I did not die at an early age. As kids, my sister and I dreamed of who we wanted to marry when we got older. My dream was to marry a teacher or a pilot. Frank is both. I wanted to finish school and I got my GED and continued on to get my associate's degree in psychology and my bachelor's degree in psychology and family studies. Even though I could not work in my own business, I get to work for God. I am so grateful for His care that gives us the desires of our hearts and that His arm is not too short to bring them to reality every day.

- 6 -

Parental Concerns Never Cease

Praise God He never sleeps, but is always watching over us even when we make dangerous decisions. My son has struggled with drugs and depression due to a life-threatening disease and other circumstances. God protected him from taking his own life and from others who were not safe people. One evening, I was awoken from sleep with a strong urge to pray for him. I prayed continually for several hours and was still unable to go to sleep. I asked the Lord to help me pray and also give me some rest. A short time later, a sense of peace came over me and I was able to go to sleep. About three days later, I had a chance to talk with my son. I asked him what had happened the night I was kept awake by God to pray for him.

My son told me he had been suffering from an ulcer in his stomach for some time. He drank some whisky and his ulcer started bleeding. With no other way to the hospital, he rode his bike as fast as he could and passed out at the door of the hospital. I do not know all of the details, but he said he woke up in the hospital with a sheet over his head and a DOA (dead on arrival) tag on his toe. That was the time I was praying. God's arm is definitely not too short. I praise God for never sleeping and always watching over us.

There have been several times I have been awoken and told to pray for different people. At least two of those times it was for soldiers in danger in the Far East. These were people I did not even know. God is so faithful to His people as well as to those of us He knows need His help. He knows our names and our needs and always sends His help right on time. His time. He is never too early or too late. I am so privileged to be a prayer partner with my Lord.

- 7 -

God's Hand in Unexpected Blessings

Frank had been working for days to get photos of our boat onto Craigslist in order to sell it. Finally, he succeeded. The next morning, we received a phone call from a man (I will call him Mr. C) who was interested, and he and his wife came to see the boat. Mr. C brought a barrel big enough to fill with water in order to run the boat motor and check its condition. Frank and I prayed that if there was anything wrong with it that God would reveal it to us.

Frank and Mr. C tried to start the motor, but were unsuccessful. Frank found that the solenoid was not working, so the prospective buyer chose to go to a parts store nearby. After putting it on, the motor still would not start. They decided to bypass the solenoid and the engine started. They let it run for a while and it ran fine. When they had shut the motor off and were taking it out of the water barrel, they noticed an oil leak on the underside of the motor. Mr. C had decided to buy the boat up until finding that problem, but Frank told him he would not sell the boat to him in that condition. Mr. C said he wanted to pray about what he wanted to do and would call Frank in the morning.

While the men were working with the boat and discussing the next step, his wife and I went into the house and visited. During the course of our conversation, I let her read the first chapter of the book I was writing. She shared her story with me and we were both blessed by our conversation. Both of us being Christians, we were able to recognize that whether they bought the boat or not, my story helped in the healing of her story. That showed me that God wanted me to write my book to help others find faith and healing after experiencing tragic events. He teaches us to overcome evil with good, which is not always easy. When our self-esteem is all but gone, God equips us with what we need in order to help ourselves and others find their value in God.

Sometimes when tragedy is at an early age or older life, experiences leave us with questions like "Where was God?" and "Why did He allow this?" After over sixty years, I now realize that because we live in a sinful world, bad things happen to all of us. Satan is very real. He is an Enemy who wants to destroy the lives of those God chooses to use for His good. God gives all of us the power to work together with Him to restore and be a part of His healing process for the world. Some will reject it while others will realize it and thrive for God and His mighty purpose for us and our stories so we can identify with a fallen and hurting world. When we can connect with the hurting, we can make a difference because we can recognize the signs and the feelings of hurt in ways that others may not.

When Mr. C called back about the boat the next day, he asked Frank what he decided to do about the boat. Frank told him we both decided, after prayer, that we could give Mr. C the boat if he still wanted it, or we could give it to the people Mr. C worked with who had a ministry of getting wounded vets back to work and gain back their dignity through restoring old boats. Mr. C decided to accept the boat. He asked Frank about our favorite charity and he told him we supported Adult and Teen Challenge. He then told Frank he would give the money he was going to use for the boat and give it to Adult and Teen Challenge.

Later, Mr. C told us about his son who had called him that morning and shared that he needed help to get off of meth, but did not know how. Mr. C then thought that perhaps he could use the money he was going to use for the boat to sponsor his son in the Adult and Teen Challenge program. What an unexpected combination of blessings occurred that only our great God could bring about!

It does not end there. Just that morning, I was crying out to God for His help. God said for me to write this book, but I had been at a standstill for days. I told God I wanted to obey Him, but I did not know what to write next. His Word says that if we ask anything in His name according to His will, He hears us, and if He hears us, we shall have whatever we ask for (1 John 5:14-15). I told God I believed Him and I needed His help to obey Him in writing this book. This is the chapter that the day unfolded. Showers of blessings as well as some wonderful new friends. Thank you, Lord. To God be all the glory! Your arm is not too short.

- 8 -

Daily Blessings Can Often be Overlooked

Many of our daily blessings often go unnoticed. I was getting ready to have morning devotions with my husband, but was feeling down that I could not do more to help my children through their times of great difficulties. I realized they needed their space to grow in the Lord without my help, which is a good thing (perhaps I still struggle with being an empty nester). It was at this stage of thinking when my phone dinged with a photo notice. There in my cell phone were several family slideshows. These come on my phone at unexpected times and are fun to watch with the music provided. I have no idea how they get there or who generates them. This gift could not have come at a better time. The tears began to flow and I blessed my Lord for His perfect timing.

As a child and teenager as well as through most of my adult life, I have considered learning music to be a pipe-dream. Several years after marrying Frank, I was able to take lessons so I could learn to play the organ. My husband knew how to play several musical instruments, but I could only play the radio or record player at that time. I was sad and always felt I was lacking this very special gift of music and proper training. My secret dream was to attend the Juilliard School of Music and learn from the best. Although a friend of mine was not associated with Juilliard in any way, her tips and training for me were priceless. My friend is the best pianist I have ever known, is very accomplished, and takes her teaching to the highest degree (she taught in Germany, Canada, and the United States).

One day, I told my friend I was trying to learn my technique better, but found it difficult due to my constant struggle with dyslexia. Still, I never gave up, and I am grateful the Lord gifted me with a strong will and determination. These positive attributes have helped me succeed in accomplishing most anything I choose to do (used rightly, a strong will and determined attitude can bless others and help to inspire others to always do their best). She was surprised when she realized how strong my interest was and invited me to ask her if I needed help from time to time. In 2023, she offered to give me a few sessions in technique. I was delighted that she would do that for me! To this day, she continues to help me to have a better understanding of scales, cords, and arpeggios. She told me, "Not knowing technique is akin to being a Christian without a Bible."

I also think that having this training without practicing regularly is like having a Bible and not reading it and practicing doing what it says daily. She has no idea that she is a huge answer to my lifelong prayer and my used-to-be pipedream. Every time I remember how God's arm is not too short, I can only say "Wow!" and praise Him. I will always strive to do my very best for Him and not forget to honor those He uses as contributors to His answers and their faithful obedience to Him. All praise to my Lord and to my friend who is His obedient servant.

- 9 -

God Shows Up in Unexpected Places

As I begin to write this chapter, I am praying God will show me what to write. I know God is everywhere and in everyday life, but I think of those times when we do not know what to do next. When there seems to be no real answers to difficult situations. We all have them, and somehow, they always seem to work out. That is God's miracle, for sure.

My husband and I have been praying for my children for over thirty years. They have struggled with homelessness, illness, building relationships, having mutual respect for one another, and a host of other things. These things are common in many homes, yet there seems to be no answers. After many years of prayers that seem to have gone unanswered, COVID hit and took its toll on the family. My daughter and her family were still in the throes of COVID when they were forced to evict their home. My husband and I were not able to take all of them into our home at once. They had five adults and one seven-year-old child living in their home at the time. Two of them went to a friend's house, two lived in the car, and one adult and the seven-year-old lived in our home temporarily.

After a few days, the two living in the car needed to come over and wash clothes. They stayed late into the evening until their laundry was finished. They were pretty loud with strong opinions as were some of the other family members. My husband and I had a group discussion with all of them on the principles of our home and why we were not able to take everyone in. The dad, who lived in the car with his adult daughter, was feeling like no one was caring for him. We were able to tell him that we really did care, but the yelling and disrespect they had for each other just had to stop. I told the dad of something I had heard years ago, "When people are arguing, the one with the loudest voice has the weakest argument." The dad looked at his daughter and said, "That is us." I realized then that they both wanted to change for the better.

The mother needed help cleaning out their trashy car and just could not get along with her daughter. I told the daughter that she needed to respect her mother and help her even though she had already done her part. I told her

God Shows Up in Unexpected Places

when I was young, my mother said to take the time to help the other person finish, too, whenever there was work to be done and I had finished mine. This shows love for one another. She tried, but it was not long before she came to me in tears and told me she just could not work with her mother.

I went to the mother and asked to hear her side. It turned out they both thought they had mutual agreement, but each of them had a different idea of what the agreement was. Pretty soon, they both were in the blame game. I told both of them that we are to be kind to each other and then asked each of them in turn if they loved the other. Both said yes. Once that was settled, I told them that all of them, including the seven-year-old and the dad, were the ones who made the mess together and that they should be a team and clean both cars together.

Praise the Lord! For the first time, they all worked together as a team without fighting, yelling, blaming, or accusing one another. That was a miracle. God's hand is not too short. The dad finally realized that he was loved and our relationship was healed. Another miracle. God also helped me to see him in a different light and really understand his heart, hurt, and needs. God gave me understanding beyond anything I could imagine. After over thirty years of seemingly unanswered prayers, I saw firsthand how faithful God is and how He really does work all things together for good to them that love God to them who are called according to His purpose. (Romans 8:28)

God changed the perspective of my daughter's family as well as ours. The dad's health currently is not good and is becoming very serious. We are not capable or qualified to meet his needs for he is disabled and needs in-house care 24/7. My husband and I do the best we can and are praying fervently for God's continued intervention. I have had three or four chances to discuss the plan of salvation and the importance of accepting Jesus as Lord of his life. They have mostly been positive conversations. The choice is up to him now, and I trust God will continue to lead him through His Holy Spirit. I am sure there is more to come on this story. These circumstances and resolutions showed me how God works all things out for the good of those who love Him and are called for His purpose. God's arm is not too short even when working with difficult people and tough circumstances.

- 10 -

The Power of Prayer is Always Active

The power of prayer is always active in our daily lives. Through the trials of life, God is always very faithful. Through His Word, He commands us to keep praying without quitting. Always be in an attitude of prayer or singing songs and hymns to Him; it is a vital command. He is our Lord and the Keeper of our souls. As I grow in my walk with God, He teaches me to trust Him more each day. He also wants us to have our desires fulfilled, too. All in His time, not necessarily ours, yet sometimes it is His will to provide when, where, and how we desire. That is His choice since He knows how He wishes to build our faith or teach us to wait on His perfect timing and why. Who are we to argue with our Maker?

My road has not always been an easy one. Without the prayer support of friends, family, strangers, acquaintances at my Sunday school class (my spiritual family who are faithful in prayer and works of love), my dear sweet husband, and my Lord, I would not have survived. All of you hold me up by His divine grace, for which I am very thankful.

Through the strain of taking on some of the struggles that come with being a true follower of Christ, God always supplies what I need to keep me going so I can finish the task or tasks He has put before me. My husband has been a tremendous blessing to me. God gave me a wonderful loving husband who is sensitive to God's leading and faithful in doing what the Lord convicts him to do.

Throughout the difficulties we encounter in taking others into our home, Frank takes time to do things to take care of me as well as himself as I do for him. Sometimes we have an impromptu lunch, a walk, or even a nap whenever we get a few minutes or hours alone so we can recharge for the rest of the day. Sometimes, he sets boundaries so I do not overwork myself. He has boundaries that protect his personal space as well as our personal space and our lives as a couple. We both agree to these boundaries and cherish our lives together. We have mutual love and respect for each other. We each have our own personal devotions as well as regular times of reading devotionals and the Bible together, praying together, and playing and laughing together throughout the day. These things do not cost money and come with the rich blessings of our loving God.

We have our struggles as any other married couple, but with being faithful in prayer and honest about our own shortcomings without blaming one another, we are able to build each other up in the Lord and move on in the joy of the Lord. These are our choices. Happiness is not something to be searched for, it is a choice. When we choose to accept Jesus as our Lord, we choose to be faithful followers of His even though life can be very rough and bumpy. God is faithful to be there when we need Him; He never leaves us or walks away to leave us on our own. When He is silent, ask Him to show you what He is up to. While you are enduring the silence, praise Him for His faithfulness and rest in His peace. Quit worrying and fretting. Remember, God has this; His arm is not too short. Start praising Him when the doubts come and watch for your unexpected surprise. Resist the devil and he will flee away from you.

So, praise our faithful God believing in His upcoming answers in the face of fear, doubts, and uncertainty. Rejoice in God's victory and enjoy your day. Practicing this daily has changed my life and caused me to be able to see the evidence of God's hand at work. Obeying God's manual for our lives is key in showing God we really love and trust Him. This is coming from a woman who was raised with fear, distrust, doubt, and more. Growing up without the love and acceptance of a father and doubting the love of my mother made it difficult to consider the love of a heavenly Father. My self-worth came from God and the grace to truly believe in the God of my salvation. God is the daddy I never had and always hoped for. I am God's miracle. Praise His name forever.

- 11 -

From Tragedies to Blessings

God uses tragedies to bless us and others when our lives have been shattered. God never wastes a tear. There have been members of my family as well as myself who have experienced some horrific things.

My mother was molested by her father many times. When Grandma did not want her husband's affections, she would tell him, "Well, there is always your daughter." Mom was forced by her mother to prostitute herself as a teenager so that she could get cigarettes for her mother. I do not remember why she told me those things; with the exception to warn me once about my grandpa who was coming to visit. She said he wanted to sleep with me and that if he came near me, I was to hit him on the head hard with the hammer she put under my pillow. I was about eight or nine years old at the time. I did not know what to think nor did I understand why I was to hurt Grandpa.

When I was a young teen, life for me was difficult. One uncle offered me money to go to bed with him. I was devastated when I told Mom what he said. There were men in and around where my family lived who were not safe. I begged Mom to adopt me out, but she never would. I did not think I belonged with this family. That is when she dropped a bombshell on me.

The reason she would not adopt me out was because she had a child by her father. Her baby boy was born when she was about sixteen years old. She had been sent to a home for unwed mothers and was forced to adopt him out. After she married my dad two years later, she tried to get her son back, but Dad would not allow it. When Mom was about eight, her mother had a baby girl who was also adopted out. Mom had always wanted a sister and remembered holding her sister Irene's little hand just before she was taken away. What heartbreak I must have caused my mother when I begged her to adopt me out. I had no idea what she had gone through in her life.

I have tried to locate my brother many times to no avail. I left my name and phone number in his birth records at Booth Memorial Home for Unwed Mothers in case he ever wanted to find his birth family. His adoption was a closed adoption, so after they were opened, I was able to leave the information he needed to find me if he chose to, in the event he ever discovered that he was adopted. He is loved even though I have never met him. Mom named him David Allen, but who knows if the adoptive parents changed his name. He would be in his mid- to late seventies by now. I never quit hoping to find him. Rather than disrupt his life, I chose to make his search easier if he chose to do so.

- 12 -

God Sends His Angels to Guard Us

One day when my husband was at work, I had to drive to the hospital in Portland. I asked my daughter, Buffie, to go with me. She agreed. As I was getting in the car to go pick her up, my car was suddenly surrounded by four men. The one closest to me said, "We will be with you." Then they were gone just as suddenly as they had come. I was amazed and did not know what to think. I thanked the Lord, picked up my daughter, and drove to Portland. At one point, I got lost and needed directions. I turned into a service station and got directions, but as my daughter and I were walking back to my car, a very angry man was coming after us for reasons unknown. I told Buffie to get in the car fast. The man was hesitant to pursue us. He was looking around as though the men I had seen earlier were standing guard around us. That was when I realized God had sent His angels to protect us.

There was another time when I was driving down the freeway and was trying to pass a large semi. I was unable to because a white car was in my way and just stayed there in the lane beside the back of the truck. Had the car moved out of my way, I would have been in the direct path of the tire that blew on the semi, which would have hit my small car and, most likely, totaled it and me. I believe to this day that God caused me to see that car. After the truck blew the tire, I looked to see what happened to that car. It was gone; not in any lane and nowhere to be seen. God's protective care is everywhere.

Scriptures tell us that God's angels are messengers He sends to us. Another day while driving home, there was an older couple walking along the road and looked as though they could use a ride. I told the driver to stop and see if they needed a ride. The couple got in and we proceeded to drive in the direction they had been walking. The man did not say anything, but the lady and I started a conversation about the eruption of Mt. Saint Helens. I mentioned that the coming of the Lord was soon. The lady replied, "Sooner than you think." Then, she said, "You can let us out now." I asked her if she wanted us to take them somewhere, but she said, "No, you can let us out here." As soon as they got out of the car, they both disappeared. The driver and I looked at each other in disbelief. We looked everywhere for them. There were no cars, shrubs, or trees around. They simply vanished before our eyes.

Many years later, I was reading *When Angels Appear* by Hope MacDonald. One of the stories was about a truck driver who had a very similar experience, only this driver went to the nearest police station and reported it. He was then told that he was the seventh person to have the same thing happen. This also happened just after the eruption of Mt. Saint Helens. I gasped in surprise. That was a time in my life that I had been questioning my salvation. God's arm is not too short and His timing is always perfect.

- 13 -

Seeking God Has Great Rewards

One Sunday, Frank and I picked up our granddaughter and great-granddaughter to bring then to church with us. The past week had been a rough time for my granddaughter, Ella (as she requests to be called). Ella had been living temporarily in a woman's shelter with her seven-year-old daughter. Recently, they were transferred to an apartment through a transition agency. There, she was counseled in her financial management and particulars of household management.

Ella had been working two full-time jobs while also trying to manage getting her daughter to school and having a babysitter after school. There came a week when Ella's ride to school was not available and her babysitter was sick. Ella was forced to stay home with her daughter. In tears, she let her daughter watch TV as she went to the restroom and cried out to God. She told Him she did not know what to do. She had to let go of one job and needed to know which one. The next day, Ella received a phone call from one boss who said they needed someone more dependable and they were letting her go. That same morning, Ella received another phone call from her other boss who told her they were increasing her hours and she would not have to work weekends. They would also work with Ella concerning school and babysitters.

Ella was so full of gratitude to God. She said, "If anyone missed God's answer to my prayers and did not see God's hand in it, here is your sign." What a blessing to hear how God blessed her! Frank and I have been in constant prayer for them for years. God is truly there when we need Him and always right on time. God's arm is definitely not too short or too slow.

- 14 -

God's Protection is With Us Wherever We Go

In the early 2000s, Frank and I went with some friends to their resort in Lake Tahoe, Nevada and had a great time while we were there. We decided to take a last trip around the crater before we left to go home. As we started around the crater later that afternoon, we were on a ridge with very steep slopes on each side. We could see the road ahead of us where the undergirding had fallen away as there had been an earthquake earlier that day. It was dangerous to cross it, so we had to find a way to turn around before we reached it. It was not long before we found a side road to a campground and were able to go around. God's grace is amazing.

It was a beautiful day when it came time to go home. As we traveled home, we were on a two-lane road. The traffic was moderate to heavy; we were in the right lane, but both lanes were full. Suddenly, we saw a car in our lane coming straight at us. We had nowhere to go and could only watch, as if in slow motion, as the car came closer. At the last moment, the other driver of the car went around us on our right. We had just passed a tree and all I could say was, "Lord," as my thoughts were for those who were in the car. Just up the road, we stopped at a rest area. Some people who had been a few cars behind us came in and we asked them if there had been an accident. They said no and I praised God for our protection and for those in the car. God's arm is not too short and is very quick and accurate.

- 15 -

God Turned a Crash into a Blessing

Tuesday, December 20, 2022, my husband and I were traveling down the road when the driver behind us rear-ended us. Frank and I both ended up with a whiplash. The person who hit us was very distraught, so I tried to calm her down as much as I could. She was shaking so violently I feared she could have been in shock. We tried to get each other's information, but were not able to get it all. In the process of getting her calmed down, I asked her if I could pray with her. She agreed. I was able to lead her through the prayer of salvation to comfort her. She was very thankful.

Frank and I saw our chiropractor for several months after the accident. She sent both of us to massage therapy. Frank improved more rapidly than I. Our chiropractor sent me to a cervical surgeon in Portland. After many x-rays and MRIs, I had surgery on May 4, 2023. I stayed two days and nights in the hospital because my pain level was difficult to manage. After being discharged, Frank and I went home. The ride home was long and very tiresome. May and June were a time of intense pain and discomfort I have never experienced before. I have many allergies that create a problem when it comes to pain control and other medications. I praise God every day for His protective care of me.

- 16 -

Watching God Working Strongly in My Family

My prayers have been for the salvation and spiritual growth of my family. Even though some have serious illnesses, they need to trust fully in God. If I help them too much, they depend on me rather than their Savior, Jesus. After the accident in December of 2022, I have not been able to help them as much. They wanted to live with us at one time. Frank and I prayed and asked God what to do, and He told us it was too much for us. We realized we could not take them in. This meant they would be living in their car.

How does God expect this caring sensitive mother to watch her sick children go through this? I had to choose to obey God or help them anyway. The only choice for me was to obey my Lord. As Frank and I continued to pray, God just said, "Watch." I watched and cried rivers of tears.

I am now seeing the miracles God is doing. I am seeing them become more responsible and caring. Their family unit is becoming stronger when it comes to caring for each other's needs, self-centeredness is becoming more cohesive, and the actions and attitudes of all of them shows the amazing grace of God at work.

All of this change is coming together quickly, and I am just amazed at God's wonderful hand and how He chooses to keep me out of the way. Frank and I prayed and asked God what we can do to help my family; His answer was to watch. What I realize today is what I am watching is God changing the lives and attitudes of very strong-willed people. To Him be all the glory. That is an amazing miracle! Miracles are amazing, but the most amazing to me is when He performs a miracle in a person's life.

They are still struggling and may for a while, but God's arm is not too short as He continues to carry them when they cannot carry themselves.

Through all of this, I have learned a faith and solid trust in God's constant presence and loving active grace. God never leaves us or forgets us when we are down. He is just a prayer away and He always knows what we need before we ask.

Prior to COVID, I asked God to teach me the faith of Abraham that was counted to him as righteousness.

When I pray dangerous prayers, I may have to walk a very difficult path with God in order to arrive at the destination He has for me. I see His continued grace and His faithfulness that never ends. I am forever grateful for answered prayers and God's ongoing love, held closely in His everlasting arms.

- 17 -

When God Calls, He Provides

I love the King James Version of the Bible. The Book of Psalms teaches me that my times are in God's hands. He will instruct me and teach me in the way which I should go. God Himself will guide me with His eye and His eye is always upon me. How wonderful and comforting that is as I go through life. Many times, life has been full of situations I do not always understand. When I wonder where God is and why He is allowing these things to happen, I am reminded that His eye is always upon me and that His nature is for good. He works all things out for the good of those who love Him. He calls us according to His purpose.

I have watched many people go through terrible sufferings that prepare them to cope with other things life brings their way. If these people seek to understand God's heart in the process of their suffering, they will find the wisdom of God that He is building their lives upon. I believe it is through my sufferings God has caused me to become a better person. Blaming God or others for our difficulties just keeps us stuck in our pain and hinders our growth and maturity in life. We need to be strong, healthy-minded people ready to be our best for God and others in this world. This kind of wise maturity only comes when we choose God's wisdom. When people need to fix a car or anything else, the best place to start is the manual from the maker. Our Maker's instruction manual is God's Word. This Book has been the go-to for centuries and is perfect for all situations.

We do not toss aside the car manual because we do not understand it; we seek out someone who can interpret it for us. If we lack understanding of the Bible, we can ask God for understanding and He will give it to us. Sometimes, God speaks directly to us through our thoughts or we suddenly see the answer. Pastors, Bible studies, or just reading the scriptures are some ways to get help finding the answers. If we ask God, we are promised we will receive it in His time, not always ours. Sometimes, I have had to wait years to understand why God has allowed me to go through such hardships. In time, I was able to realize it was God's presence that helped me through.

We learn as humans to comfort others by the way we are comforted. For some, we learn compassion for those who have no comforter. Jesus is our very present help in our times of trouble. We can be like Jesus with skin on to others who hurt because through our experiences, we understand where others may not. It amazes me how God uses ordinary people like me and you to be His hands and feet. We all have different ways we can help each other. Our job is to do it and get out of our own pain by helping others grow in wisdom and understanding with us. After all, we are all in this together. In this way, we can also grow in our trust and faith in God.

- 18 -

Jesus's Example of Trust in His Father

The angel of the Lord encampeth round about them that fear him.

Psalm 34:7 (KJV)

God knows those who are His. He watches over and guards those who call on Him and those who are vulnerable and have no voice, who are weak and desperate. He walks beside all of us and holds each one of us by His righteous right hand. What more security could anyone want? He carries us when we have no strength left to stand or even take the next step. I know firsthand this is true because that has been true in my life every day. Sometimes, I have not always realized His presence, but the fact is He has never left me, especially when I felt abandoned. His truth and faithfulness can always be counted on.

God has a perfect plan for each of us. He always completes what He starts. When I am ready to give up, He sends me encouragers. I am so very grateful. One day while I was trying to write, I was feeling discouraged. I was finding it hard to write and accomplish more than I have in this past year. I was trying to keep up with a deadline I had not even established yet. I was just trying to finish the book God asked me to write as soon as I could so I could be diligent with my time for Him. All the while, I was careful to wait for His leading in all that I was writing. This is God's assignment for me and needs to be done His way and in His time, not mine. I set down to write one thing and am inspired to write something completely different. He guides me with His eye.

Jesus was obedient to His Father when God sent Him into a sinful world as a tiny, helpless baby. He trusted His Father to restore Him to His Father's side when His mission was complete. He obeyed everything His Father said, even going to the cross when God had to turn His face away from His obedient Son when He took our sins on Himself. He trusted His Father's righteousness and willingly gave up His life as His mission demanded so we could be reconciled to the family of God and joint heirs with Him. This is the highest form of trust and obedience. I strive to be obedient and trusting of God's wisdom above my own any day. It was not easy for Jesus and it is not easy for us either, but a servant is not greater than his Master. We are to be like Him. Jesus chose to be God's conduit for salvation and restoration, and we are to be His conduit for a lost world.

Acknowledgements

To God's Holy Spirit who inspired me with words to express the inexpressible for me.

To my husband, Frank, for his patience, prayers, and loving support through it all.

To my Open-Heart Sunday School class and their encouragement and many prayers.

To my children, Buffie Marie and Brian Thomas, who were part of my stories and my blessings through some of the toughest times of my life. Thank you.

Thank you to the staff of Xulon Press for your help, encouragement, and prayers.

And thank you to Alicia Smock for coaching me as an author and helping me develop my story.

The Afterlook of the Ice Storm.

Waking up to Ice.

After the Fire

Roof damage from the tree falling.

Tree falling down in the yard.

The look of breaking down the tree.

About the Author

Cindy grew up in a welfare family with a single mom and seven children. As the second child, she felt unloved and unaccepted. In her mid-teen years, she decided to get away from it all and got married at sixteen. However, after eighteen years with an alcoholic and unfaithful husband, she filed for divorce.

After the years of tragedy and heartbreak, Cindy went through a vocational rehab program and was given a new start. She went to a community college and finished her GED. She then went on to earn an associate degree in psychology. Later, after meeting and marrying her current husband, she enrolled in the local Christian college Western Baptist College (now Corban University). She graduated from their adult studies program with a bachelor's degree in psychology and family studies.

Due to a number of previous surgeries, she was unable to work or continue her education. She now works for the Lord, assisting those God sends into her life. She says, "There is no pay financially, but the benefits are out of this world." Through her education in psychology, she was able to heal a great deal emotionally. After thirty-five years of marriage, God called her to write her life's story and in the process of writing, God showed her answers to her lifelong questions and healed her completely both spiritually and emotionally. She hopes this book will help others know that God is always there for us in all circumstances. He restores what Satan has stolen and gives us understanding, new purpose, and helps us see that our self-worth comes from Him. His purpose in everything is to prepare us to be a conduit for Him to reach a lost and hurting world for the glory of God.

She says, "To God be all praise and glory. My heartache and painful past are Gods to use; thus, fulfilling His purpose for me in this life."

I would love to hear how this book has helped you! Feel free to leave a comment at:

miraclesthroughtragity@gmail.com

Printed in the USA
CPSIA information can be obtained
at www.ICGtesting.com
LVHW050404310124
770384LV00001BA/10